The National Intelligence Strategy of the United States of America

Foreword

I've often said publicly that we are facing the most diverse set of threats I've seen in my 50 years in the intelligence business. That's true. It's also true, however, that we are better organized to face these threats than we were 13 years ago. We have strengthened and integrated our Intelligence Community (IC) in the decade since 9/11, supported by the *National Intelligence Strategy* (NIS).

This, the third iteration of the NIS, is our guide forward for the next four years to better serve the needs of our customers, to make informed decisions on national security issues, and ultimately, to make our nation more secure. We face significant changes in the domestic and global environment and must be ready to meet 21st century challenges and to recognize emerging opportunities. This guidance is designed to propel our mission and align our objectives with national strategies. The NIS provides an opportunity to communicate national priority objectives to our workforce, partners, and customers—from the policy maker, to the warfighter, to the first responder, to our fellow citizens.

To navigate today's turbulent and complex strategic environment, we must: (1) Execute our mission smartly and identify ways to better leverage the substantive work of our partners and potential partners; (2) Continue to integrate, transform, and strengthen the IC's support to national security; (3) Protect privacy and civil liberties and adhere to the *Principles of Professional Ethics for the IC*; and (4) Adapt to changing needs and resources and innovate to provide unique anticipatory and strategic intelligence.

We have seen a great deal of success in integrating intelligence in the five years since our most recent NIS, with both high-profile operational achievements and significant enterprise improvements. Together, we must build on our successes and mitigate risks, guided by this updated strategy. We must continue to evolve as an integrated Community, advance our capabilities in technology and tradecraft, and push for improvements in both mission and enterprise management, through initiatives such as the IC Information Technology Enterprise.

We have crucial work before us. Senior policymakers depend on us to enable them to make wise national security decisions and Americans count on us to help protect the nation from attack, while increasing transparency and protecting their privacy and civil liberties. We must provide the best intelligence possible to support these objectives; doing so is a collective responsibility of all of our dedicated IC professionals and, together with our partners, we will realize our vision.

Thank you for your dedication to our mission and to the security of our fellow citizens as we continue this journey together.

James R. Clapper
Director of National Intelligence

Purpose

In support of the *National Security Strategy*, which sets forth national security priorities, the *National Intelligence Strategy* (NIS) provides the IC with the mission direction of the Director of National Intelligence (DNI) for the next four to five years. IC activities must be consistent with, and responsive to, national security priorities and must comply with the Constitution, applicable statutes, and Congressional oversight requirements. The NIS should be read along with the National Intelligence Priorities Framework and Unifying Intelligence Strategies to inform and guide mission, as well as planning, programming, and budgeting activities.

Organizational Framework

The NIS has four main components, described as follows: (1) the *Strategic Environment* section portrays the global national security milieu; (2) the *Mission Objective* section describes key mission priorities and expected outcomes; (3) the *Enterprise Objective* section describes resource and capability outcomes needed to enable mission success; and (4) the *Implementing the Strategy* section provides broad organizational guidance to meet the NIS's requirements.

Our success as a Community is measured as much by our defense of America's values as it is by the execution of our intelligence mission. What follows is a succinct depiction of the IC's Mission and Vision, which serves as the foundation for the Mission and Enterprise Objectives. Fundamental to all of these elements are the *Principles of Professional Ethics for the IC*.

IC Mission

Provide timely, insightful, objective, and relevant intelligence to inform decisions on national security issues and events.

IC Vision

A nation made more secure by a fully integrated, agile, resilient, and innovative Intelligence Community that exemplifies America's values.

Mission Objectives

Strategic Intelligence
Anticipatory Intelligence
Current Operations
Cyber Intelligence
Counterterrorism
Counterproliferation
Counterintelligence

Enterprise Objectives

Integrated Mission Management
Integrated Enterprise Management
Information Sharing and Safeguarding
Innovation
Our People
Our Partners

Principles of Professional Ethics
for the Intelligence Community

As members of the intelligence profession, we conduct ourselves in accordance with certain basic principles. These principles are stated below, and reflect the standard of ethical conduct expected of all Intelligence Community personnel, regardless of individual role or agency affiliation. Many of these principles are also reflected in other documents that we look to for guidance, such as statements of core values, and the *Code of Conduct: Principles of Ethical Conduct for Government Officers and Employees*; it is nonetheless important for the Intelligence Community to set forth in a single statement the fundamental ethical principles that unite us and distinguish us as intelligence professionals.

MISSION. We serve the American people, and understand that our mission requires selfless dedication to the security of our nation.

TRUTH. We seek the truth; speak truth to power; and obtain, analyze, and provide intelligence objectively.

LAWFULNESS. We support and defend the Constitution, and comply with the laws of the United States, ensuring that we carry out our mission in a manner that respects privacy, civil liberties, and human rights obligations.

INTEGRITY. We demonstrate integrity in our conduct, mindful that all our actions, whether public or not, should reflect positively on the Intelligence Community at large.

STEWARDSHIP. We are responsible stewards of the public trust; we use intelligence authorities and resources prudently, protect intelligence sources and methods diligently, report wrongdoing through appropriate channels; and remain accountable to ourselves, our oversight institutions, and through those institutions, ultimately to the American people.

EXCELLENCE. We seek to improve our performance and our craft continuously, share information responsibly, collaborate with our colleagues, and demonstrate innovation and agility when meeting new challenges.

DIVERSITY. We embrace the diversity of our nation, promote diversity and inclusion in our workforce, and encourage diversity in our thinking.

Strategic Environment

The United States faces a complex and evolving security environment with extremely dangerous, pervasive, and elusive threats. The IC remains focused on the missions of cyber intelligence, counterterrorism, counterproliferation, counterintelligence, and on the threats posed by state and non-state actors challenging U.S. national security and interests worldwide.

Key nation states continue to pursue agendas that challenge U.S. interests. China has an interest in a stable East Asia, but remains opaque about its strategic intentions and is of concern due to its military modernization. Russia is likely to continue to reassert power and influence in ways that undermine U.S. interests, but may be willing to work with the United States on important high priority security issues, when interests converge. The IC spotlight remains on North Korea's pursuit of nuclear and ballistic missile capabilities and its international intransigence. Iran's nuclear efforts remain a key concern, in addition to its missile programs, support for terrorism, regime dynamics, and other developing military capabilities. The potential for greater instability in the Middle East and North Africa will require continued IC vigilance. Finally, continued IC vigilance will be required to maintain global coverage of conflicts as they arise and potentially threaten U.S. interests.

Violent extremist groups and transnational criminal networks threaten U.S. security and challenge the U.S. both in the homeland and abroad. Al-Qa'ida, its affiliates, and adherents, continue to plot against U.S. and Western interests, and seek to use weapons of mass destruction if possible. The actions of transnational criminal organizations have the potential to corrupt and destabilize governments, markets, and entire geographic regions. The IC will increasingly serve homeland security as well as military and foreign policy objectives.

Domestic Environment. The IC faces fiscal challenges as the U.S. Government operates under tightened budgets. We must meet our mission needs in innovative ways and sustain our core competencies with fewer resources. Likewise, our customers and partners will also grapple with resource challenges. While such constraints will require the IC to accept and balance risks, addressing these challenges presents additional opportunities to enhance partnerships, information sharing, and outreach.

The U.S. will continue to face threats of unauthorized disclosures from insiders and others that compromise intelligence sources, methods, capabilities, and activities, and may impact international and domestic political dynamics. These disclosures can degrade our ability to conduct intelligence missions and damage our national security.

Global Environment. Global power is becoming more diffuse. New alignments and informal networks—outside of traditional power blocs and national governments—will increasingly have significant impact in economic, social, and political affairs. Resolving complex security challenges will require the IC's attention to a broader array of actors. Private, public, governmental, commercial, and ideological players will become increasingly influential, both regionally and virtually. The projected rise of a global middle class and its growing expectations will fuel economic and political change. Some states and international institutions will be challenged to govern or operate effectively.

Many governments will face challenges to meet even the basic needs of their people as they confront demographic change, resource constraints, effects of climate change, and risks of global infectious disease outbreaks. These effects are threat multipliers that will aggravate stressors abroad such as poverty, environmental degradation, political instability, and social tensions—conditions that can enable terrorist activity and other forms of violence. The risk of conflict and mass atrocities may increase.

Small, local actions can have disproportionate and enduring effects. Groups can form, advocate, and achieve goals—for political, social, and economic change—all without central leadership. Identifying, understanding, and evaluating such movements will be both a continuing challenge and an opportunity for the IC.

Technology. Technology is constantly advancing, bringing benefits and challenges. Technological developments hold enormous potential for dramatic improvements in individual health, employment, labor productivity, global communications, and investment.

Technology will continue to be a catalyst for the rapid emergence of changes difficult to anticipate or prepare for; these forces can test the strength of governments and potentially jeopardize U.S. citizens and interests overseas. Technological advances also create the potential for increased systemic fragility as foreign governments and non-state actors attempt to leverage new and evolving technologies to press their interests.

Natural Resources. Competition for scarce resources, such as food, water, or energy, will likely increase tensions within and between states and could lead to more localized or regional conflicts, or exacerbate government instability. In contrast, prospective resource opportunities beyond U.S. borders and the potential for the U.S. to meet anticipated fossil fuel requirements through domestic production are likely to alter dramatically the global energy market and change the dynamics between the U.S. and other oil producing nations.

Introduction to Mission Objectives

The seven Mission Objectives broadly describe the priority outputs needed to deliver timely, insightful, objective, and relevant intelligence to our customers. Intelligence includes foreign intelligence and counterintelligence. The Mission Objectives are designed to address the totality of regional and functional issues facing the IC; their prioritization is communicated to the IC through the National Intelligence Priorities Framework.

IC Customers

- The President
- National Security Council
- Heads of Departments and Agencies of the Executive Branch
- Chairman of the Joint Chiefs of Staff and senior military commanders
- Congress
- Others as the DNI determines appropriate

Source: National Security Act of 1947, as amended

Three Mission Objectives refer to foundational intelligence missions the IC must accomplish, regardless of threat or topic:

- *Strategic Intelligence*—inform and enrich understanding of enduring national security issues;
- *Anticipatory Intelligence*—detect. identify, and warn of emerging issues and discontinuities;
- *Current Operations*—support ongoing actions and sensitive intelligence operations.

Four Mission Objectives identify the primary topical missions the IC must accomplish:

- *Cyber Intelligence*—provide intelligence on cyber threats;
- *Counterterrorism*—understand and counter those involved in terrorism and related activities;
- *Counterproliferation*—counter the threat and proliferation of weapons of mass destruction;
- *Counterintelligence*—thwart efforts of foreign intelligence entities.

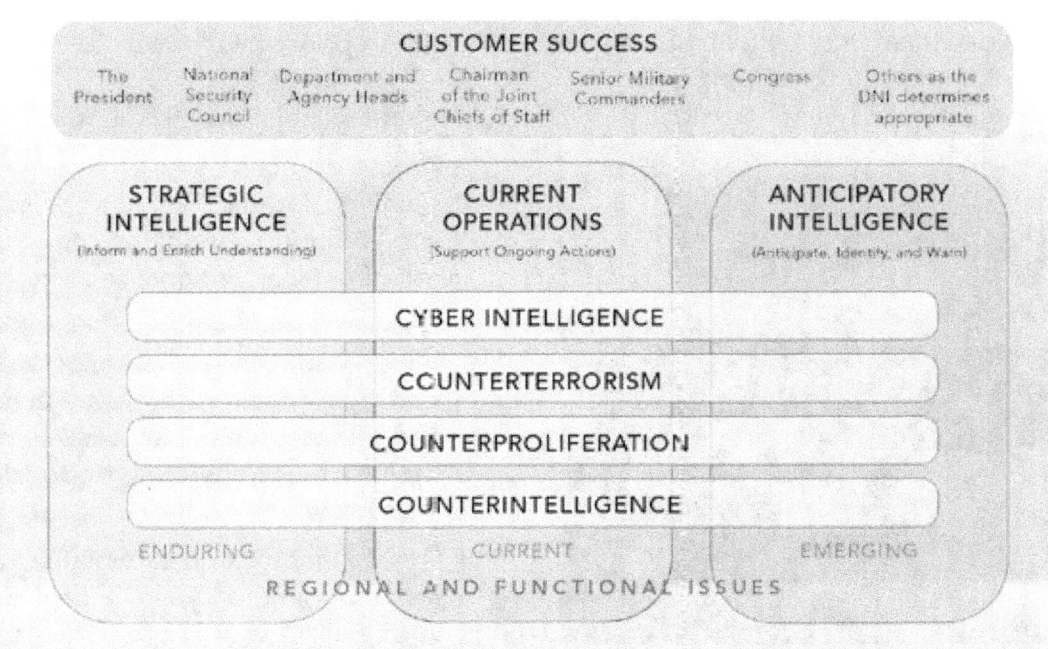

1 **Strategic Intelligence:** Provide strategic intelligence on enduring issues to enrich understanding and enable decision advantage.

Strategic intelligence is the process and product of developing deep context, knowledge, and understanding to support national security decision-making.

The foundation for strategic intelligence is in understanding the histories, languages, and cultures of nations and non-state entities, their key leaders and opponents, their objectives and concerns, as well as natural resources, technology, and transnational issues. The IC masters vital national intelligence issues through research, knowledge development, outreach, and tradecraft in order to provide deep context for a wide variety of policy and strategy communities.

To meet this objective, the IC will:

- Deepen understanding of the strategic environment to enable IC customers to pursue national security, mission- and issue-specific goals;

- Access and assess foreign capabilities, activities, and intentions to provide IC customers with greater insight and certainty;

- Provide in-depth and contextual objective analysis and expertise to support U.S. national security policy and strategy.

2 **Anticipatory Intelligence:** Sense, anticipate, and warn of emerging conditions, trends, threats, and opportunities that may require a rapid shift in national security posture, priorities, or emphasis.

Anticipatory intelligence is the product of intelligence collection and analysis focused on trends, events, and changing conditions to identify and characterize potential or imminent discontinuities, significant events, substantial opportunities, or threats to U.S. national interests.

The complexity, scale, and pace of changes in the strategic environment will test the IC's ability to deliver insightful and actionable intelligence with the fidelity, scope, and speed required to mitigate threats and exploit opportunities. The IC will expand its use of quantitative analytic methods, while reinforcing long-standing qualitative methods, especially those that encourage new perspectives and challenge long-standing assumptions. With evolving intelligence requirements, anticipatory intelligence is critical for efficient IC resource allocation. The IC will improve its ability to foresee, forecast, and alert the analytic community of potential issues of concern and convey early warning to national security customers to provide them with the best possible opportunity for action.

To meet this objective, the IC will:

- Create capabilities for dynamic horizon-scanning and discovery to assess changing and emerging conditions and issues that can affect U.S. national security;

- Deepen understanding of conditions, issues, and trends to detect subtle shifts and assess their potential trajectories, and forecast the impact on U.S. national security thus generating opportunities to alert or warn;

- Develop integrated capabilities to create alerts within the IC and to provide timely and relevant warning to our customers.

3 Current Operations: Provide timely intelligence support to achieve operational and national security goals.

Intelligence support to current operations, whether collection, analysis, counterintelligence, or intelligence operations, occurs in almost all IC organizations and cuts across almost every topic addressed by the IC. Intelligence support to current operations is characterized by the immediacy of the support provided. In addition to being responsive, this support also shapes future operations and investigations.

The IC will adapt to evolving operational requirements, maintain the robust support customers expect, and further enhance capabilities. As the IC facilitates whole-of-government efforts to take action against terrorists and transnational organized crime, address cyber threats, and respond to emerging crises—from geo-political to humanitarian—it will also need to support policy imperatives such as the rebalance to the Asia-Pacific region and transition of the allied mission in Afghanistan. Faced with a wide spectrum of operations in support of military, diplomatic, and homeland security activities, the IC will prioritize its efforts and mitigate risk, operate in denied areas, balance forward presence with robust reach-back, and provide operational resiliency to more fully integrate intelligence with operations.

To meet this objective, the IC will:

- Provide actionable, timely, and agile intelligence support to achieve and maintain operational decision advantage;

- Integrate and collaborate with diverse partners to maximize the effectiveness and reach of intelligence capabilities in support of operations;

- Conduct sensitive intelligence operations to support effective national security action.

4 Cyber Intelligence: Detect and understand cyber threats to inform and enable national security decision making, cybersecurity, and cyber effects operations.

Cyber intelligence is the collection, processing, analysis, and dissemination of information from all sources of intelligence on foreign actors' cyber programs, intentions, capabilities, research and development, tactics, and operational activities and indicators; their impact or potential effects on national security, information systems, infrastructure, and data; and network characterization, or insight into the components, structures, use, and vulnerabilities of foreign information systems.

State and non-state actors use digital technologies to achieve economic and military advantage, foment instability, increase control over content in cyberspace, and achieve other strategic goals—often faster than our ability to understand the security implications and mitigate potential risks. To advance national objectives, customers increasingly rely upon the IC to provide timely, actionable intelligence and deeper insights into current and potential cyber threats and intentions. The IC also provides needed expertise to defend U.S. Government networks along with other critical communications networks and national infrastructure. To be more effective, the IC will evolve its cyber capabilities, including our ability to attribute attacks. The IC will focus on identifying trends and providing the context to improve our customers' understanding of threats, vulnerabilities, and impact.

To meet this objective, the IC will:

- Increase our awareness and understanding of key foreign cyber threat actors—including their intentions, capabilities, and operations—to meet the growing number and complexity of cyber-related requirements;

- Expand tailored production and dissemination of actionable cyber intelligence to support the defense of vital information networks and critical infrastructure;

- Expand our ability to enable cyber effects operations to protect the nation and support U.S. national interests.

5 Counterterrorism: Identify, understand, monitor, and disrupt state and non-state actors engaged in terrorism-related activities that may harm the United States, its people, interests, and allies.

The dynamic and diverse nature of the terrorist threat will continue to challenge the U.S. and our interests and will require continued emphasis on targeting, collection, and analysis. The IC supports the national whole-of-government effort to protect the homeland from terrorist attack, disrupt and degrade terrorists who threaten U.S. interests abroad, counter the spread of violent extremist ideology that influences terrorist action, disrupt illicit financial and other support networks, and build counterterrorism capacity at home and overseas. Our government and our partners must anticipate, detect, deny, and disrupt terrorism wherever and however it manifests against U.S. interests. The IC will continue to monitor this threat to protect our nation, provide warning and assess the strategic factors that may enable future terror plots.

To meet this objective, the IC will:

- Conduct innovative analysis that supports disruption of terrorist actors posing threats to the U.S. and our interests;
- Provide insight to mitigate the spread of violent extremist ideology;
- Anticipate new and developing terrorist threats and explore opportunities to counter them;
- Bolster resiliency and build adaptive capability to counter terrorism at home and abroad.

6 Counterproliferation: Counter the threat and proliferation of weapons of mass destruction and their means of delivery by state and non-state actors.

The intelligence requirements and challenges related to countering the proliferation of weapons of mass destruction (WMD) are increasing. The IC will support objectives for countering the threat and proliferation of WMD and their means of delivery as well as WMD-related materials, technology, and expertise. The IC will work with partners inside and outside the U.S. Government to better understand, detect, and warn on foreign WMD capabilities, plans, and intentions; thwart WMD acquisition and employment; and inform U.S. policies and initiatives.

To meet this objective, the IC will:

- Develop capabilities and inform U.S. policies and efforts to dissuade or prevent states from acquiring WMD-related technologies, materials, or expertise or from reconstituting former programs;
- Advance our understanding of established state WMD programs to inform U.S. counterproliferation decisions, policies, and efforts to disrupt, roll back, and deter use;
- Support interagency efforts to secure global stockpiles of weapons of mass destruction and warn of and prevent the transfer of WMD-related materials, technology, and expertise to terrorists, extremists, or other non-state actors;
- Improve U.S. capabilities to anticipate and manage crises and support integrated U.S. Government responses to mitigate the consequences of WMD use or loss of state control.

7 Counterintelligence:

Identify, understand, and mitigate the efforts of foreign intelligence entities to compromise U.S. economic and national security.

A foreign intelligence entity is any known or suspected foreign organization, person, or group (public, private, or government) that conducts intelligence activities to acquire U.S. information, block or impair U.S. intelligence collection, unlawfully influence U.S. policy, or disrupt U.S. systems and programs. The term includes foreign intelligence and security services and international terrorists.

The U.S. faces persistent and substantial challenges to its security and prosperity from the intelligence activities of traditional and non-traditional adversaries. Foreign intelligence entities relentlessly target the U.S. Government, the private sector, and academia to acquire national security information and to gain economic, diplomatic, military, or technological advantage.

IC elements will identify emerging technologies that can be leveraged by our adversaries to compromise classified information and assets, and develop and adopt robust mitigation strategies. Counterintelligence activities must be integrated into all steps of the intelligence process.

To meet this objective, the IC will:

- Understand, anticipate, and penetrate increasingly sophisticated foreign intelligence entity capabilities;
- Develop and implement capabilities to detect, deter, and mitigate insider threats;
- Stem the theft and exploitation of critical U.S. technologies, data, and information;
- Neutralize and/or mitigate adversarial attempts to exploit U.S. supply chain and acquisition vulnerabilities.

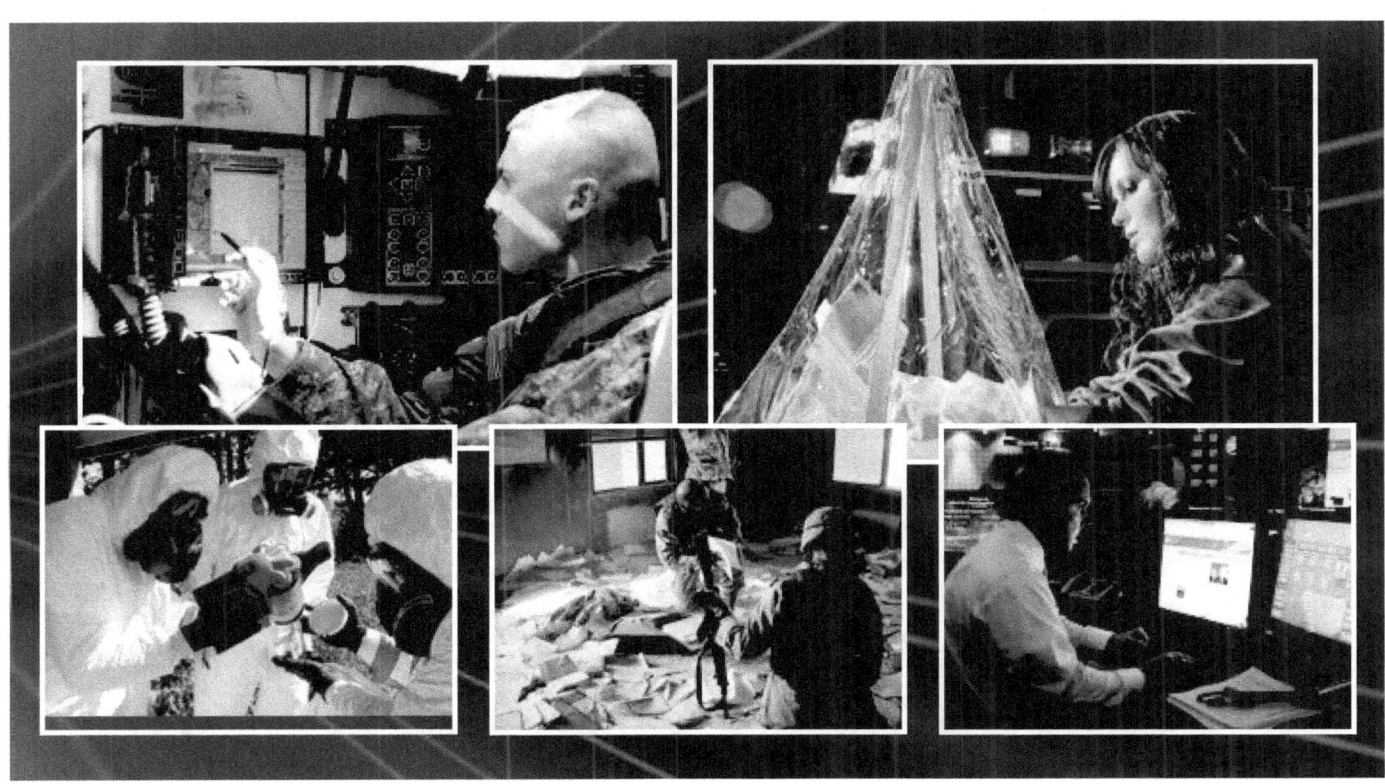

Introduction to Enterprise Objectives

Accomplishing the seven NIS Mission Objectives depends on achieving six Enterprise Objectives, which describe the resources and capabilities that are essential to fulfilling the Mission Objectives.

Two Enterprise Objectives focus on enterprise integration while optimizing resource management and decision making:

- *Integrated Mission Management*—optimize capabilities to achieve unity of effort;
- *Integrated Enterprise Management*—improve IC integration and interoperability.

Four Enterprise Objectives describe our strategy to build a solid foundation of key capabilities and capacity:

- *Information Sharing and Safeguarding*—improve collaboration while protecting information;
- *Innovation*—improve research and development, tradecraft, and processes;
- *Our People*—build a more agile, diverse, inclusive, and expert workforce;
- *Our Partners*—improve intelligence through partnership.

The Enterprise Objectives address both mission and enterprise integration and rest on the *Principles of Professional Ethics for the IC*.

1 Integrated Mission Management: Optimize collection, analysis, and counterintelligence capabilities and activities across the IC to achieve unity of effort and effect.

Integrated mission management is the strategic prioritization, coordination, and deconfliction of intelligence activities to align the interdependent disciplines of collection, analysis, and counterintelligence.
- Collection activities are responsive to and inform analytic requirements.
- Analytic activities produce intelligence judgments, identify intelligence gaps, and provide the basis for guidance to collectors.
- Counterintelligence activities complement collection and analytic activities and identify vulnerabilities of intelligence sources, methods, and activities.

Effective mission execution requires flexible, responsive, and resilient efforts to appropriately share knowledge, information, and capabilities across organizational boundaries. The IC will increase integration and collaboration across the Community to meet customer needs efficiently and effectively. In doing so, the IC will strike a balance between unity of effort and specialization within each discipline and function, using the best of each to meet mission requirements. Intelligence products will be appropriately tailored and classified at the lowest possible level.

Analytic, collection, and counterintelligence professionals, supported by coordinated governance, joint processes, and improved capabilities, will collaboratively work together to define and solve problems.

To meet this objective, the IC will:

- Leverage cross-IC, multi-disciplinary expertise and the full range of IC capabilities to jointly define and anticipate intelligence problems, develop options

for action, and understand tradeoffs for implementing solutions;
- Strengthen and integrate governance bodies to optimize resources and manage risk;
- Foster joint IC planning, targeting, tasking, and assessment processes to coordinate intelligence activities and promote continuous improvement;
- Drive integrated investment decisions and the delivery of multi-disciplinary, integrated capabilities to provide optimal solutions for mission success.

2 Integrated Enterprise Management: Develop, implement, and manage IC-oriented approaches to improve integration and interoperability of IC enabling capabilities.

Integrated enterprise management is the strategic coordination of IC business practices to optimize resource management and enterprise business process decision making.

Effectively managing enterprise resources enables the IC to fully execute its mission efficiently. Specifically, the IC will seek solutions that increase efficiencies in areas such as continuity, security, acquisition and procurement, finance, facilities, and logistics. IC-wide performance evaluation and data-driven reviews—aligned to strategy and budgets—will strengthen performance, enhance oversight and compliance, and lead to unmodified audit opinions, improved results, and lower costs. The IC will promote information security, share timely intelligence with our partners, and educate customers on proper use and handling of classified information.

To meet this objective, the IC will:

- Advance a personnel security infrastructure that supports a one-Community approach through continuous evaluation and

- Pursue acquisition and procurement strategies and processes across the IC that enhance the cost-effectiveness and efficiency of procuring common-use products and services;

- Implement IC enterprise financial standards, processes, tools, and services that leverage both government and industry best practices;

- Mature strategy-based performance and evaluation across the IC to support proactive, balanced, and informed IC decision making;

- Leverage existing and future IC facilities and physical infrastructure to support joint-use functionality and improve energy efficiency;

- Adopt a risk management approach to continuity of operations efforts to provide an uninterrupted flow of national intelligence in all circumstances;

- Continue to implement approaches to provide appropriate transparency, protect privacy and civil liberties, and enhance oversight and compliance.

3 Information Sharing and Safeguarding:
Enhance, integrate, and leverage IC capabilities to improve collaboration and the discovery, access, retrieval, retention, and safeguarding of information.

> The Intelligence Community Information Technology Enterprise (IC ITE) transforms agency-centric information technology to a common enterprise platform where the IC can easily and securely share technology, information, and capabilities across the Community.

Mission success depends on the right people getting the right information at the right time. Improving our information sharing and safeguarding capabilities, as mutually reinforcing priorities, requires strengthening our people, processes, and technologies. The IC will continue to identify and address information sharing gaps and coordinate efforts to reduce duplication across the IC Information Technology Enterprise to yield better results more efficiently.

In addition to recognizing the responsibility to provide intelligence and the growing demand to make information available across the IC, the IC will enhance safeguards to protect information and build trust among partners. An integrated information sharing environment, dedicated to protecting privacy and civil liberties, allows the IC to carry out the mission, protect against external and insider threats, and maintain the public trust.

To meet this objective, the IC will:

- Consolidate existing and future information technology requirements into an effective and efficient IC information technology infrastructure to enable greater IC integration, information sharing, and safeguarding;

- Provide the IC workforce with discovery and access to information based on mission need to deliver timely, tailored, and actionable information;

- Integrate enterprise-wide information, as appropriate, to enhance discovery, improve correlation, and enable advanced analytics consistent with protection of privacy and civil liberties;

- Strengthen and synchronize security and data protection standards for new and existing intelligence information systems based on policy-driven interoperable approaches and attribute-based access to provide a trusted and secure IC-wide information environment;

- Promote a culture that embodies, supports, and furthers responsible information sharing respectful of privacy and civil liberties.

4 Innovation: Find and deploy new scientific discoveries and technologies, nurture innovative thought, and improve tradecraft and processes to achieve mission advantage.

Innovation begins with a commitment to research and development as the seed for breakthroughs in science and technology. In order for innovation to provide results, the IC will further develop, support, and foster intellectual curiosity and creative problem solving. The IC must accept that initial failures may lead to successes and be willing to take calculated risks for high-value results when a rational basis for the risk is demonstrated. The IC will leverage innovation wherever it is found, incorporating scientific breakthroughs and cutting-edge technologies for mission excellence. The IC will extend innovation to our daily work by embracing new processes and automation to streamline the business aspects of intelligence.

To meet this objective, the IC will:

- Conduct and leverage basic research and maintain core independent research in the most sensitive applied and social sciences, technologies, and mathematics arenas to achieve breakthrough results;

- Transition creative ideas and promising innovations to improve intelligence services and processes across the IC;

- Strengthen and unleash the innovative talents of the workforce to accept risk, improve tradecraft, and embrace new technologies and processes.

5 Our People: Build a more agile, diverse, inclusive, and expert workforce.

Inclusion describes a culture that connects each employee to the organization; encourages collaboration, flexibility, and fairness; and leverages diversity of thought throughout the organization so all individuals can excel in their contributions to the IC mission.

Workforce planning is a framework addressing the total workforce balance (civilian, military, and core contract personnel) to ensure the IC has the right people with the right skills in the right place at the right time to accomplish the mission in high-performing teams and organizations.

Diversity considers, in a broad context and in relation to the mission, all aspects that make individuals unique and America strong—including race, color, ethnicity, national origin, gender, age, religion, language, disability, sexual orientation, gender identity, and heritage.

The IC workforce is united in protecting and preserving national security, which could not be accomplished without a talented workforce that embraces the IC's core values and *Principles of Professional Ethics for the IC*. To this end, the IC will continue to attract, develop, engage, and retain a workforce that possesses both the capabilities necessary to address current and evolving threats and a strong sense of integrity. Even with constrained budgets, the IC will make long-term strategic investments in the workforce to promote agility and mobility throughout employees' careers. Special emphasis is needed to recruit, retain, develop, and motivate employees with skills fundamental to the success of the intelligence mission, including foreign language, science, technology, engineering, and mathematics.

The IC needs effective tools for workforce planning, transformational learning programs, skills assessment and knowledge sharing, joint duty and other experiential assignment opportunities, and the resources to encourage and facilitate work-life balance.

All employees are accountable for cultivating a performance-driven culture that encourages collaboration, flexibility, and fairness without the fear of reprisal.

To meet this objective, the IC will:

- Shape a diverse and inclusive workforce with the skills and capabilities needed now and in the future;

- Provide continuous learning and development programs based on a mutual commitment between managers and employees to promote workforce competency, relevance, and agility;

- Nurture a culture of innovation and agility that advocates the sharing of ideas and resources adaptable to the changing environment, and promotes best practices across the IC;

- Provide a workplace free of discrimination, harassment, and the fear of reprisal, where all are treated with dignity and respect and afforded equal opportunity to contribute to their full potential.

6 Our Partners: Strengthen partnerships to enrich intelligence.

Partners consist of elements working to protect U.S. security interests, including U.S. military, our allies, foreign intelligence and security services, other federal departments and agencies, as well as state, local, tribal governments, and private sector entities.

The Community's partnerships are fundamental to our national security. Our partners are force multipliers, offering access, expertise, capabilities, and perspectives that enrich our intelligence capacity and help all of us succeed in our shared mission. The IC will deepen existing partnerships and forge new relationships to enhance intelligence and inform decisions.

Our approach to strengthening partnerships will align with broader national policy guidance and harmonize partner initiatives across the IC through policies, procedures, and practices that clearly delineate roles, responsibilities, and authorities. In working with the array of government, foreign, military, and private sector partners, the IC will remain cognizant of, and dedicated to, protecting privacy and civil liberties and maintaining the public trust.

To meet this objective, the IC will:

- Increase shared responsibility with and among, and incorporate insights from, all partners to advance intelligence;

- Develop an enterprise approach to partnership engagement to facilitate coordinated, integrated outreach;

- Deepen collaboration to enhance understanding of our partners and to effectively inform decisions and enable action.

Implementing the Strategy

The IC is an integrated intelligence enterprise working toward the common vision of a more secure nation. The NIS provides the overarching framework to accomplish the mission and achieve the vision. The IC will implement the NIS consistent with its statutory authorities under Congressional oversight.

The DNI and IC elements work together in an integrated fashion to execute the NIS. Functional managers monitor the health of important intelligence capabilities. Mission managers examine all facets of collection, analysis, and counterintelligence against specific areas of concern across missions. Program managers scrutinize how funds are executed. IC enterprise managers align support functions to enable each mission. The IC elements recruit, train, equip, and conduct intelligence missions. Inspectors General, legal counsel, and privacy and civil liberties officers ensure proper compliance and oversight.

The Office of the Director of National Intelligence provides the IC with overarching guidance and coordination. IC elements execute their missions consistent with their statutory authorities. Finally, it is the responsibility of all members of the IC workforce to understand how they contribute to the IC mission and execute their specific role to the best of their ability and consistent with the protection of privacy and civil liberties.

DNI
Serve as Principal Intelligence Advisor.
As principal intelligence advisor to the President, the DNI must ensure intelligence addresses threats to national security. The DNI establishes the IC's strategic priorities and sets forth the enabling capabilities needed for mission success in the NIS.

Set Strategic Priorities for the IC.
The NIS, in concert with the *National Security Strategy* and the National Intelligence Priorities Framework, represents the IC's mission priorities. The DNI informs Congress of significant priority realignment and activities.

Align the National Intelligence Program.
The NIS serves as the DNI's mechanism to align the National Intelligence Program and guide the reporting of resource expenditures and performance to Congress. Additionally, the National Intelligence Program is coordinated with the Military Intelligence Program and the DNI's joint annual planning and programming guidance for the IC.

IC Elements
Align Strategies, Plans, and Actions.
The mission and enterprise objectives in the NIS shall be incorporated and cascaded into C e ement strategies and plans. IC elements and functional managers will facilitate an integrated approach to these objectives to achieve the IC's mission.

Inform Resource Allocation.
The NIS will inform decisions about programs, budgets, policies, and acquisitions to develop and sustain capabilities. IC elements and program managers will reflect NIS objectives in their annual strategic program briefs and will articulate their intentions to mitigate risks in their annual planning and programming activities.

Measure Outcomes.
The execution of the NIS objectives requires constant and consistent evaluation. IC elements will provide information through existing processes to clearly illustrate how they have performed against NIS objectives and the IC Priority Goals, which measure progress against enduring national security issues. Measuring progress against the NIS is crucial to improving overall IC performance.

Conclusion

The NIS supports intelligence integration and the IC's mission to provide timely, insightful, objective, and relevant intelligence to inform decisions on national security issues and events. The IC must fully reflect the NIS in agency strategic plans, annual budget requests, and justifications for the National Intelligence Program. The DNI will assess IC element proposals, projects, and programs against the objectives of the NIS to realize the IC's vision of a nation made more secure by a fully integrated, agile, resilient, and innovative Intelligence Community that exemplifies America's values.

"The Intelligence Community exists to
provide political and military leaders
with the greatest possible decision advantage.
We understand, now more than ever,
that the best way to accomplish our goal is thorough
integration of all national intelligence capabilities."

James R. Clapper, Director of National Intelligence

2014 National Intelligence Strategy Roadmap

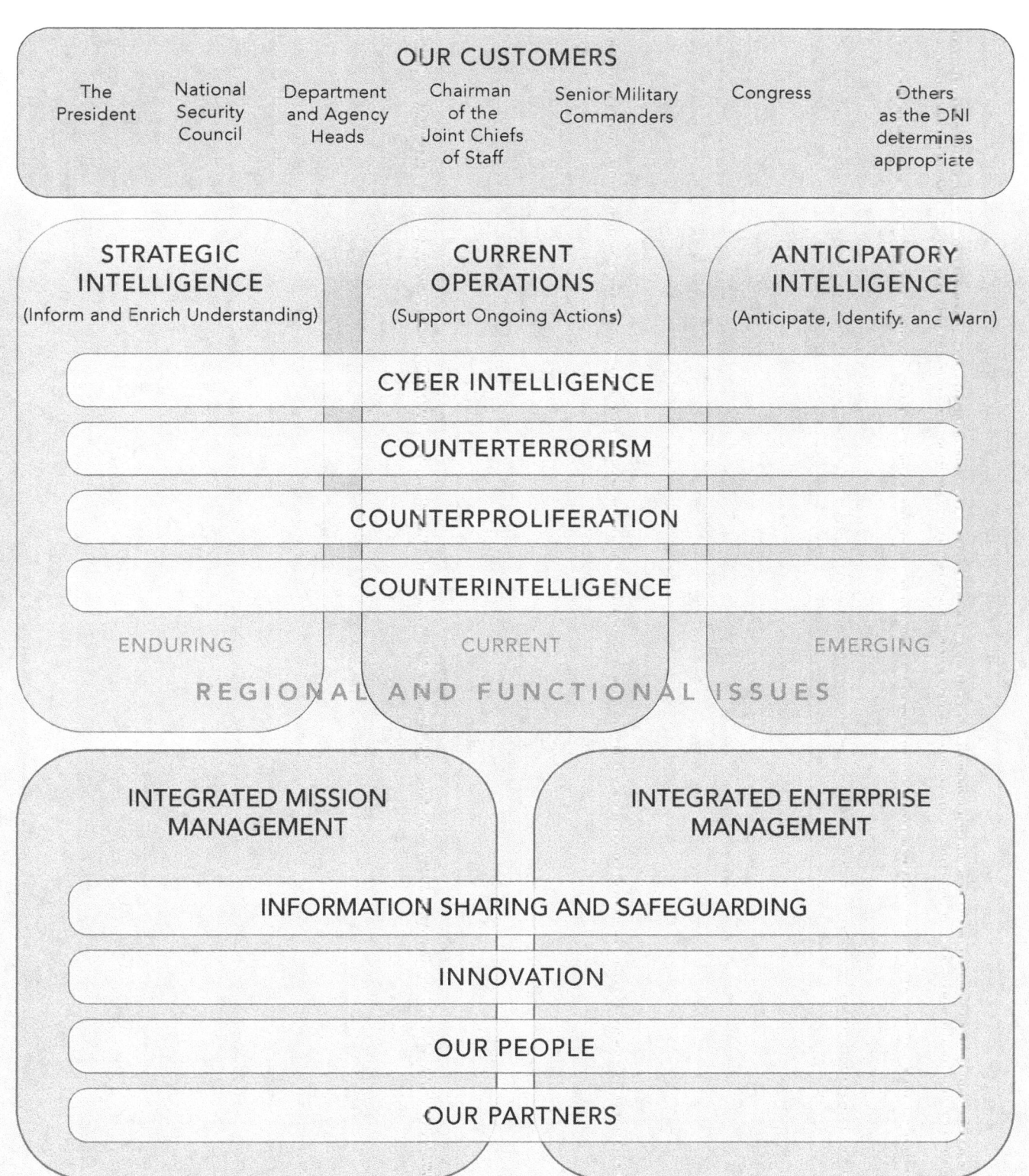

OUR CUSTOMERS

| The President | National Security Council | Department and Agency Heads | Chairman of the Joint Chiefs of Staff | Senior Military Commanders | Congress | Others as the DNI determines appropriate |

CUSTOMER SUCCESS

MISSION OBJECTIVES (Support Customer Success)

| STRATEGIC INTELLIGENCE (Inform and Enrich Understanding) | CURRENT OPERATIONS (Support Ongoing Actions) | ANTICIPATORY INTELLIGENCE (Anticipate, Identify, and Warn) |

CYBER INTELLIGENCE

COUNTERTERRORISM

COUNTERPROLIFERATION

COUNTERINTELLIGENCE

| ENDURING | CURRENT | EMERGING |

REGIONAL AND FUNCTIONAL ISSUES

ENTERPRISE OBJECTIVES (Enable Mission Success)

| INTEGRATED MISSION MANAGEMENT | INTEGRATED ENTERPRISE MANAGEMENT |

INFORMATION SHARING AND SAFEGUARDING

INNOVATION

OUR PEOPLE

OUR PARTNERS

Principles of Professional Ethics for the IC

Page Intentionally Left Blank